DEFINING LIFE

Surita Venter

DEFINING LIFE

Copyright© 2024 Surita Venter

All rights reserved. No part of this book may be reproduced in any form, except for the inclusion of brief quotation in review, without permission in writing form, from the author/publisher.

ISBN: 978-0-7961-7281-5

Contact the Author at suritav@gmail.com

Cover design and typesetting by Wade Hunkin
Printed and bound in South Africa by: PRINT ON DEMAND

Contents

Purpose	1
Introduction	5
The Power of Words	9
From Darkness to Light	17
Shadows of doubt	27
Beyond the Pain: A Journey of Recovery	35
Restoring Honour and Truth	43
Turning Point: A Family's Financial Strain	51
Yesterday's Farewell, Tomorrow's Embrace	61

Purpose

For so many years this book was an idea. It started off with the idea to be written as a fiction book; a story in the eyes of the writer with an imaginary timeline, written by someone else with the knowledge of what she has heard from me or read in notebooks I gave her. But I soon realized that this would not work as reading it back, it did not reflect the purity of the situations or people. It left a sour taste in my mouth. It sounded like a fiction story with exaggerated events; no true purpose or lesson; no true help or advice; no point.

So I stopped for years, not even thinking about it. My life went on; my journey took turns to different countries, and the book became a memory of what would have been. Then I arrived in the UAE. Thinking that it would just be a short stay and just work, I tackled every day as if work and play was all there was.

At work I had the honour to meet Jasmine. She quickly became someone who reminded me I don't need to prove anything to anyone and that I am worthy as I am. She guided me to stand up for myself and take time to care for myself.

I started coaching netball to gain some stability in life, and that's where I met Kulsum.

She saw straight through me. She could see that I was meant for more than just surviving; I was meant to shine and share the stories I know. This meant I had to remember it all and with her guidance and support, we managed to sit and dig deep to open up memories and events I have forgotten about. She became more than a mentor; she became a friend and took time from her busy schedule to challenge me, ask questions and made me see what my purpose was in life. She shone a light on my ideas and helped me to trim it to the true meaning of what the dream was right at the beginning. She saw my heart. So, with a clear direction and rested spirit, this book started off and continued to grow.

With the belief of these two people, and the understanding of how my mind works, the purpose of the book took hold. The situations will be 100% true, but to protect families, names were changed. The hope is that this book will show events that lead up to terrible situations, but also show how it was dealt with and what was learned from it.

It is my honest opinion that there are many people out there that go through difficult situations alone because they think it will be a burden to others. So, I hope this reaches those people for I know everyone needs someone in their lives to help and guide them, a shoulder to cry on, or a safe space to back off. (Like the previously mentioned people were to me).

In saying all this, I dedicate this book to Jasmine, Kulsum and the God who has always been my protector and saviour. May this book help you the same way they helped me. May you find comfort in the words of others.

PURPOSE

Introduction

The choices we make compile our whole existence.

From drinking milk in the morning to attending your least favourite lecture; from choosing a bottle of water over a coffee in the afternoon at work, to adding an extra spoon of sugar in your favourite breakfast cereal. From painting your bedroom wall an odd colour to drunk dialling your crush.

You take a plethora of decisions, make choices, and bear the consequences. Choices are everywhere, despite your parents making most of your decisions for your better and brighter future. Since early childhood you have learned to make decisions based on the options placed strategically in front of you.

The choices you make and the decisions you take have a lasting effect and impact on your life. They condition how you live life and thus put a bar of distinction between you and everyone else. Every path you take in life results from a series of choices you have made. Whether or not you notice it, your present choices shape your future paths.

In certain circumstances it is not about what you have done, but what happened to you and although you cannot always control things that come your way, you always have the choice about how you will react to it. So even in difficult situations, somewhere there will be a choice you need to make.

So, whether you decide to go to college or travel to a foreign country alone - it is your choice. It has always been your choice. The past is unalterable, yet it offers you an insight on the mistakes you have made. The present is a gift you need to make the best of, and the core of your future comprises every decision you have ever taken.

We cannot undo the past, but we can always learn from it. Choices are the building blocks of our lives and despite all the mistakes one makes, keep in mind that every new day brings with itself new opportunities and a whole new world of choices.

Remember that the choice is yours. It has always been.

INTRODUCTION

The Power of Words

As I'm sitting here thinking back to the time when I was 21, I completely understood the emotion Zoe is going through. There is always a time in all our lives where we hear something and say that it will never happen to us. The thing is, anything can happen to anyone at any point in life. Zoe saw this firsthand.

Her life always seemed on track. She managed to escape difficult situations like a lot of people. She lived from pay cheque to pay cheque and seemed in control of her life. She was a typical 21-year-old. Looking at her sitting on the couch trying to find a starting point for, what seems to be, the worst event in her life; I could feel the atmosphere change from certainty to emotional struggle. The loss she experienced changed her life, her way of thinking and doing, her way of dealing with people.

She met Liam at the age of 20. She never thought she would ever meet, what some people would call, the love of her life. Her standards were so high when it came to a guy, that it almost seemed impossible for someone like that to exist. She wanted someone like her dad. Someone that is compassionate, in control, full of love and has a huge amount of respect for the people in his life.

Liam was the brother of one of her friends, a complete introvert; completely the opposite of what she thought she would choose. There was something about Liam that tickled her fancy. Something that drew her in his direction. As she always did, she ended up just ignoring the feeling (I could fully relate to that). It didn't take long before Liam started to feel a challenge. He did not really pay attention to her, but yet there was always a feeling between them. Liam was not the type of person to take risks or put himself on the line, but sometimes Zoe thought he would glance over to her side with a slight grin. It was only when their eyes met and their hands made accidental contact that Zoe realized she fell in love.

With tears crawling up into her eyes, Zoe took a deep breath. The moment she was referring to brought a sense of happiness to the room. I could see how much it meant to her. She looked up at me and continued...

It took Liam a while before he made his actual move, because I knew he was an introvert, what happened caught Zoe by complete surprise. It happened one Friday evening at the club. As they loved playing pool, they were sitting close to the pool tables. The club was packed with music playing loudly to keep the positivity running. People were laughing, joking around and at the pool tables to could see there were some serious competitions happening between friends.

The music suddenly stopped and Bryan Adams starting singing his famous "Everything I do, I do for you." People were looking around, trying to find out why the music changed so quickly. Zoe got up to find out what was happening, and that was the moment Liam made his move. He approached Zoe and went down on his one knee to ask her to be his girlfriend. Zoe was shocked beyond words. Her heart skipped a few beats and launched herself into his arms. The cheers of the crowd made the DJ change the music back to its original state. It was the start of a beautiful life together, or so she hoped...

Zoe became quiet where she sat and looked at me. It was as if she was looking for a way out of remembering the rest.

Their time together was a fairy tale. The steal of a kiss in the back room, the look he gave her across the room that made her blush. The way he brushed his hand against hers in public. These moments made time stand still. It was as if time was giving them extra hours to enjoy the small joys of being in each other's company. It was as if time knew they would not have as much as they think.

The smile on Zoe's face filled with pain as the tears filled her eyes. I leaned over to hand her a tissue. The pain she carried was bigger than her guilt. She drifted off as she remembered the worst moment of her life. She looked away as if she could bear looking no one in the eye.

A student's life is never really easy. As a student you know finances are scary and when you wanted to pay for a university event, it would take dedication and will to save up for it. But that is exactly what Zoe did. She saved up to buy tickets for her and Liam to attend the Ms. University event. The evening started up and everything was going smoothly. Zoe could see that Liam was not really into it, but she was happy with him being there. It was close to the middle of the event that Liam received a call and came back to say that he has to leave as he had to help his brother with something. Zoe walked out with him. She was not impressed. She asked him if it was just a way to get out of the event and as the conversation continued; she told him he should leave, and that she hopes he drives into a tree.

Zoe didn't expect these words and as she recalled them, she put her face down into her hands. I could see it was the first time she admitted saying them. The horrified looked on her face was as if she pulled a trigger by accident on the person she loved so much.

For two weeks she avoided him not knowing how crucial time was. On the Friday of the end of two weeks, she went out to the club with her friends. The evening was, as always, filled with music, drinks and dancing. Zoe spoke about how her friends wanted to drive to pick up a cousin and asked her if she wanted to go along. She told them she just wanted to go to the bathroom first. She told me how she came out and looked for them, but how they left without her. This didn't bother her too much as she waited for them by hanging out with her other friends.

Zoe shuffled her feet together as if she wanted to erase all memories. She stumbled over her words as she tried to recall the events.

Something she didn't know at that moment was that she was lucky to have missed the ride along. Her friends returned in a bit of a state. They spoke about an accident they drove by. A car was hanging in the vineyard and a body was covered against one tree. Zoe didn't really pay attention to the story until the following week when her friend asked her out of the blue what the name was of her boyfriend. Zoe found it a bit strange that the question came out of the blue and asked her friend why she wanted to know. She remembered her friend closing the newspaper quickly and gave her an awkward smile. Something was not right in that moment. Zoe recalled her stepping closer and grabbing the newspaper out of her friend's hands. The article about the accident they drove by was clear and Zoe recognised the car immediately.

I looked at her as she seemed to wake up from a nightmare she was caught in. Frantic, she grabbed another tissue, almost angry at herself. She was shocked to see she was just sitting in my office; as if she didn't know she was there. I gave her a smile, and she took a deep breath as she continued.

The article spoke about how Liam must have swerved out for some cows in the road and went off the road, where his car caught the gravel and rolled. Her got thrown through the windscreen and landed in the pathway of the rolling car. He was dead on site, lying against the tree.

The memory surprised Zoe and tears rolled out her cheeks. She cried like she hasn't in a long time. She looked at me through the ocean of tears as if asking me to erase the pain. Our eyes caught and she understood. For the first time in her life she acknowledged the accident and the role she thought she played in it. The wound was open, the healing could start. In that moment Zoe realized how much those last words she said to Liam guided her life. She realized she has always blamed herself for the accident. My question threw her: "Was this your choice or did this happen to you? Was this your fault?"

PURPOSE OF THE STORY

So many times in life we tend to speak before thinking. And yes, Zoe's words didn't cause the accident, but it definitely haunted her for a very long time. Someone once said to me: *"Choose your words carefully when speaking to people, for your words might either be the last words they hear or the first words they hear in a changed life."* We don't know what the future holds for us, but holding a grudge against people will never be good for you. Time is so valuable and wasting it on remembering why you were angry in the first place takes away that valuable time. Spend the time you have with the people you love. Stop looking for reasons to be angry and rather find reasons to be happy.

As for Zoe, accidents happen, life hits us hard, regret comes quick, but a mistake doesn't define who you are. Mistakes teach us lessons; it makes us think and helps us to grow. Holding onto mistakes will sink your ship, like an anchor pulling the ship down. Hold on to the lessons, but cut the anchor of mistakes so your regret and pain can drift away.

Just like Zoe, things will not change overnight, pain doesn't go away in seconds, but cutting the line bit by bit lifts the weight one day at a time until one day it only becomes a memory in the distance.

THE POWER OF WORDS

From Darkness to Light

As I walked up to my office, I remembered the previous day's session. Ethan was waiting for me outside. A slim, strong and bubbly person. At first glance he seemed like a thrilled person; someone who has it all together, but his eyes gave away his heart. Behind his smile lied uncertainty and confusion. So many times people overcompensate for true feelings.

We sat down and I asked a very simple question: "So Ethan, who are you?" The look on his face said that this question might not have been so easy for him to answer. It threw him off-guard and brought confusion to the table as I have known him for a while now. He took a breath and smiled at me as he told me about his work, his family and his friends. He spoke about how happy he was and how great his life has been. I nodded and repeated my question. This made him look away, and he answered with one word: "Confused."

There are so many times that we all go through an 'auto-pilot mode'. For some people it is the time just before they think about giving up, kind of like living on the edge of life, hopping on one foot while clinging to a broken branch trying to not fall off the cliff and avoiding the thorns on the branch at the same time. Everything seems fine to the people around us and our view is the scenic one until someone makes us aware of the surroundings we find ourselves in. Most of these times it takes a small slip to fall down that cliff.

Ethan had lived his life on that very edge. His mind was racing thinking about my question. I asked the basic question as a follow-up: "Confused between what?"

The memories triggered quickly as he shifted around in his seat; the comfortability clear. He bowed his head and recalled the situations that brought him to my office.

For him, life always seemed so easy and moment of calamities seemed to come in three. For Ethan it was all about surviving the three and then preparing for the next three. In his mind, that was just how life was; surviving rather than living.

Ethan described himself as always being unlucky and his saving grace was hanging onto close friendships. He would do anything for validation and he spent his days trying to prove he deserved certain friendships. In all his relationships, he hovered in insecurities and this meant that he adapted and changed to fit into the box of the relationships he adored so much. The masks in his life took over, and he lost himself (which is why my question was so difficult for him to answer). After a long day of swapping masks, he would end his day, breaking down in tears behind closed doors and try to deal with the exhaustion. This all led to polydipsia (excessive drinking). Anything seemed better than the uncertainty he lived with. The problem with this temporary solution was that his drinking led to bad decisions. Ethan became someone who would do anything the crowd did just to fit in. He had no sense of control. In the state of partying, he found himself in the wrong circles and thus it meant fitting in would go against what he knew was right.

Ethan projected shame in his eyes as the memories took him back to his drunk alter-ego. I could see he didn't like that person as disgust was clear on his face.

The confession meant he was admitting to himself that his choices made him move away from his faith; the one thing that was supposed to be grounded in his life. He looked for approval in all the wrong places. He turned to me, the words of confession stuck in the back of his throat as if someone was choking him. He coughed to swallow his words. His face seemed like a baby who tasted lemon for the first time; not knowing if he should be angry, disgusted or disappointed. All the things he did while being intoxicated boiled to the surface.

Ethan described himself as being a sociable and caring person, but like everything, there is a fine line between caring about people and being a door mat people walk over. His caring nature and the unhealthy drive for acceptance turned into him becoming a people pleaser. When he was sober, he could distinguish between right and wrong, but in a gin-soaked state, 'right and wrong' became 'boring and adventurous'; a dangerous position for a people pleaser. He explained that his first line of defence that falters in this state, is his ability to keep his sexual drive intact. If a girl showed any interest, he would take it as an open invitation of acceptance. These words shocked Ethan, and he looked horrified by saying them. The shame engulfed him as he spoke about his 'activeness' in the community.

Explaining how he felt before or even during these adventures was easy for Ethan, but how he felt afterwards was a different story. Maybe Ethan thought I would judge him like most people in his life and therefore he hesitated to speak about the aftermath. He didn't want to be reminded of the destruction 'the morning after'. Our brains are wonderfully created. It has the extraordinary ability to protect us by ignoring events that hurt us. The question, however, opened the treasure chest of shame. The humble, caring person sitting in front of me, bent forward, his head in his hands and started crying like a 3-year-old boy who lost his favourite toy. I gave him a moment of silence, a moment to let go, a moment of thought, a moment of healing. He lifted his head and stared at his hands as if the weight of the memory was left behind to swim in the sea of tears in his hands.

Ethan looked at me and a light turned on in his eyes as he made the connection. The disgrace he felt sitting on the floor during his aftermath caused a build-up of depression and negativity. His glass filled up every time he tried to please others, every time he gave a piece of himself away, every time he lost himself in his drinking habits and with every mask he traded in to suit others. Ethan came to a point where his glass overflowed and that was the moment he lost himself in guilt.

The day started out as any other day for him, but the difference about that day was how it ended. As his glass was pretty full with negativity and it only needed a slight push for him to fall off his edge. It happened at work…

Ethan explained his work environment as a cage where he had to always fight to survive. He was a head server at a very popular restaurant and as they worked on commission and tips, everyone had to fight to pick up as many tables as possible. Sometimes it meant that they had to pick up tables of customers they know to be vulgar. Unfortunately, that was exactly what happened to him. He picked up a table of a couple who rarely shower people with positive vibes. He had dodged most of their comments, but as things happen sometimes, one comment caught him off-guard. Ethan stood at the table looking at the couple and a gear in his head shifted.

Ethan stared straight in front of him without blinking. He swallowed and continued…

As the restaurant is out of town, Ethan asked permission to cash up and took the first available bus back to town. He got off at the bus stop and walked over to the little shop at the fuel station. He stepped up to the counter and without thinking about the request, asked the teller for 15 double packets of paracetamol. He paid and walked out. Ethan remembered he took the first couple of packets without water as he forgot to buy some. I asked him what was going through his mind at that stage. Ethan looked at me and replied, 'nothing'.

He walked down the road, swallowing one after the other and then remembered he walked into the local pub. He asked for water and then swallowed a couple more packets. He thanked the bartender and walked out. It was moments later that he blacked out. Ethan remembered waking up in the ambulance, one of his friends sitting next to him before he blacked out again.

I stopped him at that part and asked him why he decided it was for the better to try and take his own life. Ethan explained people tend to think it's for selfish reasons; that people who commit suicide only think about themselves. However for Ethan, he saw it in another light. His reasons where because of others; to rid others from himself. He felt it would be better for others if he wasn't there. People would have a better life if he wasn't there to mess it up. He thought about all the people he hurt, all the girls whose hearts were broken, all the so-called 'friends' who always had to look after him when he was intoxicated. He felt like a burden. He felt worthless. This comment brought me back to what happened in the restaurant. I asked if he remembered what the couple said to him that set him off. Ethan broke his stare ahead of him and turned to me. "They said I'm useless and will never find people who will love me. That I'm trash which is why I work as a server. They said I will never be more than that." These words caused a silence for a couple of minutes.

After a while Ethan continued explaining how he woke up in the hospital almost choking on a tube that was pushed down his throat. His friend was sitting next to him. The doctor was busy pumping his stomach. He threw up all over the nurse; I wanted to know if that was the moment that he realized things were out of control. Ethan shook his head. It was the moment his friend told him that the three of them would get through this. (He explained that by three, his friend meant the two of them and God.)

PURPOSE OF THE STORY

Self-destruction is one of the worst things we can do. People have a tendency to want to be fully in control of everything in their lives. And when things felt out of control, it creates an abnormal spin that doesn't stop. Ethan wanted control and his self-destruction occurred when he gave himself over to alcohol. Alcohol stole parts of him. He thought he would get relief when he drank. He wanted to forget his worries, his sorrows. He wanted to feel strong, independent and on top of the world. He wanted to drown his issues. So many times you hear people say that they'll just have one drink. Often, one drink leads to two, three, five and before they know it, alcohol won the battle and as it has a contagious meaner, it makes the problems you had worse by adding extra issues, self-destruction, anxiety and depression. Alcohol freed no one from their issues, it is just the opposite, alcohol has the tendency to bind people up.

For Ethan, the abuse of alcohol created a situation where it caused him to see only one way out; suicide. When someone commits suicide the first thing people ask is: 'Why didn't they say anything?' or 'They seemed like such happy people'. Suicide isn't something people set out to do from the start. It is not the way anyone wants to leave the world, but depression, anxiety and the feeling of worthlessness are all friends that call over suicide when they reach their 100% volume.

For people who go through things like this, you are not alone. You might not see the love around you now, but God never lets us just 'be'. He never gives up on you. The result of situations like this depends all on your way of thinking. The only person who can get you out of the deep, dark hole you dug for yourself, is you. Are you willing to climb and crawl your way out? Are you willing to believe that you are worth more than what you currently feel you are? Do you want to be free?

The choice is yours. Ethan had a second chance, he had to fall flat to find out that he had support, that he was worthy and that he could do it. Learn from others and find out before that point that: **'*So are you*'**. Ethan was lucky. It could have been a completely different story had he been stripped from his second chance.

Shadows of doubt

Saladin walked into my office as a strong, confident, young man. When you look at him, you would never say that he had ever struggled with doubt in his life. It was clear that he wanted to portray a faithful man, a man that was raised with strong morals and values. Saladin's eyes gave away the overcompensating nature that his job expected from him. As he showed the set attitude of a typical defence attorney, I opted to ask basic questions. We spoke about his family, his friends and his job. He spoke about the hectic schedule he needs to keep and the crazy demands his clients have. He explained how a fine line between what is morally right and what his clients perceive as right, sometimes gets moved according to the situation. I could see that Saladin loved his job and in general, his life. It was an interesting area to dig into, so I continued asking him about his job. I could see that some confusion came to the surface when we spoke about recent difficult cases he had to attend too. It was as if he didn't like the road the conversation was heading in and the natural ways of the defence attorney came out as he sat upright. I asked him if any of the cases ever crossed the line he was so adamant to keep.

Saladin lost it. He started raising his voice venting about how the question was unfair and that I would never understand the role he has to play. He shouted about how people shouldn't judge him. I left him to vent and throw his toys out of the cot, showing no emotion or responding. It took him about 10 minutes before he settled down and took a breath. His trigger was as clear as daylight. I looked at him and repeated my question. They looked at me in silence. I could see how he froze, and it was evident that he wouldn't be able to avoid the conversation. He stood up, looked, at me and left my office.

It wasn't until about a week later that I had an unexpected visit from him again. He knocked on my office door and peered in. I smiled and stood up to greet him. He came closer and fell onto the couch that separated the door from my desk. He started by apologising for walking out the previous week. I looked at him and asked him why the question had such an impact on him. Saladin took a deep breath and told me about the first moment he could remember where the rug was pulled out from under him; the steadfast kid of 8.

It all started when he was invited to a birthday party of twins that attended the same school as him. They knew each other well and spent a lot of time together. They would spend hours playing sport, riding their bikes but he had never spent the night at their place. His mom had a strict policy on spending the night anywhere else than with family. This birthday party was a bit of a different situation. As there were a couple of kids spending the night, his mom agreed. Saladin was so excited about this.

A bit of background on Saladin:
Saladin grew up in a Christian house that taught him everything he knew about the life a Christian. His parents taught him about the relationship between him and God. They taught him the stories in the Bible. They had regular Bible studies, worship sessions and prayer groups. He learnt he could steer his boat

in a certain direction, but God will guide the winds to take him where he needs to be. He knew that what was written in the Bible is a guide on living; it is a Book of guidance. As a kid of 8, he found it difficult to distinguish between what is written as figurative, therefore certain books in the Bible were not discussed with him by his parents. But other than that, he took what he read as literal and the only truth.

The party was like any other 8-year-old's party. His memories he shared with me were very positive. He didn't go into detail about the day's activities. He just said it was fun, and the food was great. As it was his first sleepover, I asked him about the evening's activities. That memory had more detail to it and I could see that this was the memory that bothered him more. The kids all had pizza for dinner. They each took a pillow and blanket and made themselves comfortable in front of the television. Saladin was sitting on the couch. The twins' mom said she had a movie for them to watch. Saladin explained how the introduction to the movie made him feel uncomfortable, but at that stage of his life, he didn't really knew what it was about. The movie was all about Revelations. It started of with introducing the characters. At first he thought it was a boring movie, but because he was raised to be respectful, he kept quiet. The movie soon escalated into a violent and inappropriate sight for 8-year-olds. Saladin repeated twice how he asked the mom if they could watch something else. The mother paused the movie and said words that Saladin will always remember. She told him it is a story in the Bible and that it was a learning experience. Saladin didn't really want to say anything back as he could not recall his parents ever telling him that story. He sat down and continued watching. The movie showed how God's people were taken away in an instant and how the people that were left behind had to choose between getting the mark of the devil on their right hand or forehead; or be beheaded in the plain in front of all the other people.

The picture Saladin was describing made me move slightly in my seat. The graphics were uncalled for and Saladin explained in detail how people were tied down on a guillotine; others standing watching them. The vicious countdown and then the drop of the blade with the result being a head in a bucket. Saladin spoke about the screams of families looking on. He told me how he stood up again looking at the mom and asked her where the story is in the Bible. The twins' mom brought him a Bible and opened it at Revelations. Saladin stared into nothing while recalling how he read Revelations 13, which was opened for him. He read how people made their choice and how they were beheaded. The twins' mom explained that this would be what would happen someday. It was a book written for the future. She also told them it could happen at any given moment and that this meant parents could be taken away from their children or vice versa. Those words did not sit right with him. He asked her if he could please phone his mom.

Saladin held his breath without thinking about it. I put my hand on his shoulder and he jumped as if I crept up on him.

The memories he recalled about that evening seemed like it haunted him for some time. He described it as being very confused with what he thought was the Truth and what he read in Revelations. He spoke about how he woke up as a kid in the middle of the night and took his blanket with him so he can sleep on the floor in front of his parents' bed. He was afraid they would disappear like the people in the movie and he would be left behind. His life became a constant reminder of fear; fear of what's coming, fear of not understanding; fear of being left behind. I asked him what his greatest fear was and his response was that he would one day stand in front of God and be told that God does not know him.

This whole situation created doubt in Saladin's life. So, thinking back to the question I asked him in the beginning about whether there had been cases where he had crossed his moral line, it made more sense of why he flipped out about it. Saladin wiped his tears and asked me if we could continue the discussion later. I stood up and grabbed my diary. We met up in two days' time.

I waited two days before contacting him, but to my surprise he was waiting outside my office door when I arrived. He looked at me and said that he was ready to cross the bridge to get rid of the fear he had been carrying around.

It took a couple of sessions discussing the ins and outs of Revelations and making sense of how he perceived it. Although it took time, I could see a change in his way of thinking and his way of living. Saladin didn't take on cases at work out of fear anymore. He took cases where he knew he would not cross his moral lines.

PURPOSE OF THE STORY

Without us always realizing it, things might happen at a very early age and it can affect our entire lives. Sometimes we snap at people for no apparent reason or cry at the smallest things. These things happen when something triggers us. In moments like this, the best possible thing you can do is to take a step back and think about why it triggered you. Ask yourself the question of why does that upset you? Life was never and will never be easy. If life is just easy-go-lucky we don't grow, we stagnate. Most people are grounded on what they believe. If you don't believe in anything, you will fall for everything. Your boundaries will then be determined by your situation. This in itself will confuse the person you are. How can you stand for anything if you don't know what to stand for? In Saladin's case, being a lawyer needed him to believe in himself and what is right and wrong. As a lawyer, he had the ability to talk his way in and out of anything, but it haunted him, for what was right in one situation tended to be wrong in a different situation. He confused himself because his identity was confused. His legacy and the person he portrayed to others, and himself was never a true reflection of who he really was. He looked at an outline sketch in the mirror and the day's happenings filled that sketch in. He was lost, he was triggered, and he wore masks. It took time, a hard look at himself and a decision for him to become the man he believed he was. This is possible for everyone, this is possible for you, this is a personal choice...

Beyond the Pain:
A Journey of Recovery

The day I met Jenna was a very interesting and altogether busy day. Jenna wasn't your typical teenager. She wasn't the girl who made TikTok videos and worried about how many followers she could have. She didn't care if guys looked at her and were even interested in her. She actually seemed reluctant having any guy close to her.

We facilitated a week long camp for a group of teenagers from the city. Team building, some extreme activities and just pure fun was on our schedule. Needless to say, we had praise and worship sessions and self-search sessions as well.

Jenna was a girl from the second group The Ravens. They were a force to be reckoned with. They won nearly every challenge we gave them and despite being the youngest group; they went out to prove a point. The group comprised 5 girls and 5 guys, the perfect combination of brains and brawn. We challenged them with mental activities and physical activities and none of these seemed to be impossible for them.

On the second day of the camp Jenna's team had to overcome fear by getting the entire team from one end of an imaginary river to another. There were obstacles in place to hinder their progress. Some girls and some of the boys were given inabilities like hands being tied, only allowed to use one leg or being blindfolded. Jenna chose to be blindfolded. This meant that she had to be carried across. Her friend, Brian, offered to carry her. As Jenna got onto his back, I could see the unease on her face. She shifted around a bit, but held her composure. It was not until they were halfway through the river that things went all haywire. Brian slipped and grabbed hold of Jenna to avoid her falling. Jenna freaked out completely and started screaming at him. He loosened his grip and Jenna jumped off his back, crying. She ran to the bathroom. I told the other facilitator to watch the group so they could carry on. I walked to the bathroom to find Jenna sitting on the floor with her head in between her legs, shaking and crying. I sat next to her, and she grabbed me, put her head on my shoulder and continued crying. I sat with her for what seemed like an hour. She looked up at me and the look on her face told me she did not know what happened.

The rest of the day went smoothly, and we were all very excited for the evening session to start. That evening was when it all came out. We stepped into the hall for some praise and worship and Jenna took her spot at the back of the hall. We opened with some lively music and got everyone ready for a night of reflection. Our head facilitator had a talk about trust and how sometimes we get hurt by the people we trust the most. Jenna looked at me with a frightened look and I suspected that she might have remembered a moment in her life that she did not want to remember. I walked over to her. Jenna stared at the floor. I sat next to her and asked her what was going through her mind. Jenna glanced over to me and said the one thing no-one wants to hear. She recalled the time her cousin molested her.

The statement was hanging in the air that night as Jenna was avoiding the topic after she mentioned it. I decided to give her time to come to terms with what she said.

It took almost two days before Jenna came to me. It was after breakfast. I was sitting at the table outside finishing when Jenna stood in front of me and asked if she could join me. We had some free time for reflection as it was the last day of camp, so I knew it would be the perfect time to have a proper conversation without interruptions. I looked up and gave her a smile. She sat down across from me. Jenna stared at the plate on the table and after a few minutes she started telling me the story of how her cousin came to visit them for a holiday. He was older than her. She was 9 years old at that stage.

(For the purpose of this story I have decided not to go into detail about the actual event, but rather writing about the impact it had on Jenna.)

Jenna spoke quickly and vividly as she told me how her cousin came up with an excuse of curiosity and that he was just seeing what his friends were talking about. Jenna explained how she was numb and blank. She felt like a trash bag that tore and all the rubbish spilled everywhere... Useless and broken....

She took a breath and looked at me. Her eyes were filled with tears, long forgotten tears. I reached my arm over her shoulder and pulled her closer. She put her head on me and broke down. I could feel the pain she was going through. Through her tears I heard her say that it was the person she trusted most in her family and it hurt her so badly.

I asked Jenna if it happened more than once. She shook her head. This was the reason she didn't mention it to anyone, as it never happened again and thus could just be stored away as a bad memory. It was only during the team building activity that she realized that her behaviour towards men in general had a peculiar outcome. I asked her what she believed to be happening. Jenna responded that since that moment in her life she has always been weary of any male in her surrounding. Unconsciously she didn't trust any male close to her, certainly not those who are dear to her. This came out when Brian had his hands on her on that second day. The manner in which he handled her, brought back the overflow of memories she had pushed away for so long. The vivid image of her cousin on her burst through the walls she had up and all she could do was try to get away. At 18, her body was running away from the monster that was locked away for six years. Her body was screaming at her and everything inside of her was trying to protect her.

Our brains are absolutely amazing. It is a true protector. A lot of the times when something terrible happens in our lives, our brain has a tendency to block it out to protect us from pain and it is only when you're purposely trying to remember or when something triggers it, that it comes to the surface. It can be years later, like in Jenna's case. However, although the memories where locked away for Jenna, the consequences played a big part in her life. She never understood why she reacted towards men, or boys, in that specific manner. Her subconscious mind was protecting her without her knowing it.

I went on a journey of healing with Jenna. She opened up about the exact moment, the feelings, the aftermath and the consequences. She worked through every thought, every accusation and every form of blame she had towards herself and her cousin. It was not an easy journey and there were plenty of "give up" moments, but she pushed through.

The several months of healing led us to the point where we were joined in my office with her cousin. Jenna invited him to sit down with us. I asked Jenna before the meeting how much contact she had with him and she replied they saw each other often, so her inviting him didn't seem strange to him. Jenna, myself and Richard sat down. I offered both of them something to drink and stood up to pour it in. While doing this, I overheard Richard asking why she wanted him to come to my office. Jenna responded with silence and I realized how difficult the next conversation would be for her. I walked up to them and gave them each a glass of lemonade. I put my glass down and the table and asked Jenna if she wanted to start the conversation.

Jenna looked up at me and then turned to Richard. This was the moment of taking the reigns back I was waiting for. Jenna asked Richard if he remembered the holiday that he came and visited them when she was 9 years old. He nodded and then shifted in his seat. I could see he recalled something that made him a bit uncomfortable. Jenna stared at him and then told the story of a cousin taking advantage of someone he should have protected. It seemed like Jenna only took a breath when she was done. She looked away. I gave her a tissue. Richard leaned forward in his seat, lay his face in his hands and took a couple of minutes. He looked up and, ignoring me, reached his hand over to Jenna. Jenna froze. Richard put his hand on her shoulder and with that started crying. Jenna looked at him in shock. Richard swallowed his tears and all he could get out if she thought he molested her. She nodded. Richard sat back and wiped his tears away. Time stood still for what seemed like 10 minutes. Richard opened his mouth to speak, but all that came out was how sorry he was. He apologized over and over. Shaking his head, he uttered he was always looking after everyone else and never realized his own family was hurting. Jenna smiled at him. She surprised me with her response and told Richard that she had forgiven him already, but wanted to tell him so they could start again and build on a relationship they could both be proud of.

PURPOSE OF THE STORY

So many people have memories blocked away. Many individuals prefer to overlook it, hoping it will simply disappear, but have you ever responded or reacted to something or someone and then ask yourself later why?? People are very quick to say "let the past be the past" or "it's over, forget about it". The actual truth is that although your brain can block it out for you, events like that form a part of who you become and how you react to certain things. If you don't deal with it, it might form a part of you that you don't like or others see as negative. Your past will always be a part of you, but what it does to you is determined by how you deal with it. Nothing in life heals by running away from it. Now, everyone's situations will be different and maybe the relationship with you and whoever is not important to you, but what I've learnt in life is that a virus on the inside of you will keep on destroying parts of you until you do something about it. Ignoring it will not make the virus disappear.

Now for Jenna, it could have gone in a completely different direction. Richard could have denied the entire situation and that could have been the end of their relationship, but that would still have been better for Jenna, as she would have gotten it off her chest and knew exactly where they stood.

I hope that whatever you are keeping locked away will come to light and be the first step of healing so you can live a "virus-free" life.

Restoring Honour and Truth

Have you ever been in a situation where you know 100% that you are innocent, but somehow nothing you say or do can prove your innocence? My next testimony is from a man that faced the same issue. Now, some of you might think it's something big, like murder, but no, this is not a Law & Order story. In saying this, what some people might see as something small, others might experience as a huge setback in their lives.

Gilmore came to me at the age of 23. He seemed like a man that had everything together, well groomed, well dressed and well behaved. Gilmore shone positivity and light, walking into my office. At first I thought he wanted to set up a meeting for someone else. He seemed unsure of why he was even there. I asked him if he wanted to have a discussion and he smiled. He sat down and told me who he was. Gilmore came from a steadfast household. His parents taught him right from wrong. They made sure he was well cared for and educated. He studied finance and now has a financial degree. The problem was that he could not hold on to a job for very long. This has caused difficulty for him and although he is fantastic at what he does, according to his previous employers, he left each job because of feeling uncomfortable. He knew it was never the companies he worked for, but rather an uneasiness within himself. The problem was that he does not know why. He loves working with numbers, but when it comes to actual money of others, everything in his body runs away. It seemed like a past experience might have caused him doubt.

We set up some sessions, and I gave him a list of questions he needed to look at for us to continue. Gilmore took the list from me and made a promise to look into it.

About a week later we met up again. Gilmore looked a bit muddled. We sat down and I offered him a cup of coffee. He took the coffee from me and asked why those questions were given to him. I explained I knew the questions would open up some memories that were tucked away. He nodded and then started his story.

Gilmore worked for a non-profit organization when he was younger. They did camps and retreats for groups, whether it were schools or companies. As an employer of the campsite, he was put in charge of a group that came in. The facilitators ran the program that involved activities and presentations. He was there as an observer and a hand in making sure things run smoothly. He was also in charge of the tuck shop. Every day, he would fetch the petty cash from the financial officer and open the tuck shop up. The same petty cash would then be returned afterwards so she could cash it up and prepare it for the next observer to take for the other group staying there. This would continue until the groups are done and left. Her job was to make sure she cashed up the money and put in a certain amount as a float and then bank the money. In that way the books would make sense at the end of the day after stock taking. It seemed like a flawless procedure.

Gilmore stated that when he took the petty cash one morning, he realised that all the money was still in it and no cash up was done. When he asked about it, she said that she would cash up when he was done. This meant that three time slots would have gone by without a cash up, however this did not bother him as he trusted her. Gilmore took a sip of his coffee while he gathered his thoughts. He continued. He always had a Bible verse pasted on his company radio as a reminder of the goodness of God. He wanted to ask her to cash up before he took the money, but trust is earned, so he left with the money. Little did he know that it would have been a huge mistake.

After the time slot he returned the petty cash and gave the key in as he was the last person in the tuck shop for the day. The camps went well, and the campers were happy as always. He explained the vibe of the campsite as a breath of fresh air. It was a place he wanted to stay at for as long as possible. He enjoyed working there. After the campers left, the staff all had the weekend off. Gilmore and one facilitator went into town for the weekend. They went out that evening for a night on the town.

Gilmore and Felix hit the local pub for some pool and a couple of drinks. As Gilmore saved up some money, he bought most of the rounds as he knew Felix didn't really have any money. They played a few rounds of pool and even challenged two locals. Gilmore noticed Felix took a call and although the call wasn't very long, Gilmore could see that he was upset afterwards. Gilmore asked him about it, but Gilmore said it was work and they would deal with it when they returned to the campsite the next day. Gilmore didn't feel good about the reply, but as it was the first time in months they could go out, he decided to let it be and worry about it the following day.

Gilmore glanced at me and I realized that these were memories he didn't want to recall. Perhaps this was why he asked me about the questions I gave him. We sat in silence for a while and then I asked him if he was fine to continue. Gilmore responded he had never spoken about it to anyone and actually forgotten about the whole event. He took a breath and continued.

The following day Gilmore and Felix returned to the campsite. As they arrived, Felix was called to the owner's house and Gilmore went to his own. He said it felt like hours he waited for Felix to finish so he could hear what was going on, only, Felix didn't go to him afterwards. Instead, he received a radio call from the owner asking him to please go to the house. Gilmore felt like his heart sank into his shoes as he didn't know what to expect.

Upon his arrival at the house, the owner invited him in and he took a seat at the kitchen table. The owner seemed really upset and asked him if he knew why he was called in. Gilmore looked at me as stunned as I thought he would have been in that moment. Gilmore told the owner that he did not know what was going on. The owner explained to him he was there because he stole money from the company.

Gilmore stood up and walked around in my office. He seemed to struggle with the thought that he was accused of stealing money from the company. He took a few moments and sat down. I asked him how he responded to this. He shook his head. He didn't respond to the owner. He sat there and just stared at the owner as the owner carried on accusing him and told him off. The owner then started hammering him on how he could call himself a Christian and walk around with Bible verses on his radio while he steals from a non-profit organization. Gilmore said the owner never even gave him a chance to respond.

As Gilmore continued with his story, I could see how angry it made him. What would anyone do in a situation like that where you know you are innocent, but have this bully shouting at you? Even worse, diving into your character? I completely understood why Gilmore seemed so angry.

His boss eventually gave him a moment to say his piece and all Gilmore could say was that he did not know what his boss was talking about. His boss then went on saying that Felix told him he spent a lot of money the previous evening and as he knew they don't get paid a lot, the money was probably the money he stole. Hid boss also told him they would not renew his contract seeing his probation period has ended and that he should take his things and leave the premises immediately.

Gilmore got up from his seat in my office again and shook his head. At that stage in his life, he was away from any family and did not have any place to go. Luckily a friend helped him out for a couple of days before he got a bus ticket to go back to family.

After hearing the story I understood why he was so cautious working with other people's money. I knew I had to ask a very serious question that Gilmore probably did not want to hear. "Did you take the money?" Gilmore gasped at the question and then shook his head. "No."

It took us only a few sessions for Gilmore to come to terms with the fact that people would accuse you of things, because they might not want to know the truth.

I went to Google the company Gilmore was talking about and came across an article that was written a few weeks after Gilmore left talking about a lady who worked in the office that was arrested for fraud and theft. I send the article to Gilmore. He called me later that day, crying. It was the closure he needed.

PURPOSE OF THE STORY

I learned very quickly in life that people who are unhappy or uncertain about themselves sometimes go out of their way to hurt others. Toxic people don't like seeing others happy. One thing Kulsum taught me was that when others go off on you or say nasty things to you, it is more about them than about you. You will always find people in life that would rather break you down than build you up, but you don't have to listen to them or take it to heart. You know who you are; you know what you do or did and if what they are saying does not apply to you, don't take it upon yourself. I know it might be easier said than done, but if you are certain about who you are, then you have the choice of which words you take for you and which words you cast away. Words might be a double-edged sword, but it will only hurt you if you take it in. A sword is only dangerous when it cuts, you don't have to stand helpless and let everyone take a swing at you with their swords. Build your armour up, and trust yourself. Always remember that no person knows you as well as you know yourself, so if it doesn't apply to you, don't take your amour off for it to hurt you. The choice is yours.

Turning Point:
A Family's Financial Strain

As I write this book, I know people look at me and think that I must have had a very easy life. Well, maybe it's fair that I tell you a story of my own.

You are right when you think I had a stable household growing up. I have two wonderful parents and a brother that, like most, irritated the mickey out of me, but I love him dearly. I had the wonderful opportunity to see most of the provinces in South Africa, living in Mpumalanga, KZN, North West, Western Cape and Northern Cape. For many people, staying in one town for your entire childhood is a dream, as you have lifelong friends and a place you call home. Me, on the other hand, believed that staying in one place for not over 4 years at a time taught me to adjust and make the best of everything. It also taught me you have to be great full for who you have in your life as you might not have them close for very long. As bad as some may think this is, I see it differently. My parents showed me how beautiful our country is, they showed me that the country has so much to offer.

As a child, I remember my dad's company sending him to different branches all over to work and even as I got older, and he changed jobs, he always seemed to find those companies that saw the wonderful abilities he has to sort situations out and thus, no matter who he worked for, they would send him to where his abilities were needed. I truly believe this was the calling my dad had. In saying this, we learned a precious lesson in life. When you walk in God's way, you are protected, but when you go your own way, God will do what is necessary to get you back on track. This we found out the hard way.

When I was in Grade 4, 10 years old, my parents started their own business. They had it all worked out. It was a printing business, printing business cards, pamphlets, brochures, and many more. My mom started off at the house, converting one area of the house into an office. My dad was still working at Mondi. She made a name for herself in our town and my parents expanded the business and moved into town. My dad left his job and joined my mom. Yes, yes, I know people think that a married couple can't work together, but my parents are a different kind of special. They set boundaries early enough where work starts and where it ends. Their business soon grew extremely big. I still remember learning very quickly how to use the machinery and the computers. It was a joy helping when I could and learning new skills. Soon my parents had to employ others. It was a true family business. And as a kid, we had everything we needed or wanted. A big house with a pool, weekends to ourselves and money. What I didn't see was that money and an easy life is not actually what we want. As a kid it is a dream, but in the long run, not quite.

My life as a kid was exactly what I wanted it to be. Friends, sport, church, family and stability. In my eyes, I thought we would live there forever, at last a place I could call home.

My uncle from North-West came and visited us and seeing how well the business was doing and who might need the service, he had a conversation with my dad and after consideration between my parents; they went into business with him and move from the place I called home to a city I knew nothing about. I was at the end of Grade 8, my first year of secondary just finished. We packed up all the stability; I greeted people I thought I would never leave. I said goodbye to a life a so longed for to move to what was explained as "a bigger opportunity". The thirst to get more and be more. Although I've said goodbye too many before, that specific goodbye ripped a part of my heart out to keep as a reminder in a town I used to call home. The memories of the fun we had as kids, driving our bikes everywhere, causing havoc in the garden, the reluctance to get out of the pool, the constant voices of kids in the house, the forts we built in the lounge, the multiple sports we tried out, the fireworks in the street, jumping off the roof into the pool when we shouldn't, was all left behind in a bag next to the trash can to be thrown out with the other things we could not take with. Moving is hard :(

Arriving in a suburb of Klerksdorp I already had a bad feeling. But as always I was willing to give it a fair go. We arrived during a summer break in December, which meant I knew no-one, had no friends and was stuck in a small suburb with nothing more than a couple of shops and a park no-one went to. My parents said it was only temporary and that we would move to Klerksdorp as soon as we could find something there. It was the longest couple of months of my life. I remember walking down the street wondering if I would ever make any friends.

I could not wait for school to start. That first day of school, grade 9, was one day I looked forward to so much, but little did I know it would be a different kind of kid I would meet and a different type of school. Upon my arrival at school, I was taken to the head to sort out my subjects. At my previous school we could not choose subjects yet, but at the new school they chose subjects the previous year already, which meant that I was a year behind with subjects I wanted. As I have a mind for numbers, I wanted to choose Accounting, but the teacher I was assigned to, refused to teach me as I was a year behind. The head called the other teacher for accounting and he gave me a chance but I needed to catch up on the basics of the previous year on my own time. I was up for the challenge. Accounting ended up being one of my favourite subjects and the subject that granted me an A in Grade 12.

Despite the challenges I faced at school with friends and sport, my family got hit by a low blow during my Grade 10 year. My uncle withdrew from the business and left my parents with a lot of debt they could not repay. My parents ended up selling the business so they could pay all the debt. They walked away from it with no profit, blacklisted and my dad without a job. My mom was lucky enough to find an office job at the college, managing the creditors (Ironic that she worked in the line I was aiming for). Our lives took a turn for the worst. We had to move from a 5-bedroom house to a 2-bedroom townhouse. We lived on the bare minimum and while struggling, still had a brother at university. My mom worked hard, trying to keep her head above water, while my dad did odd jobs for people after struggling to find work. Money disappeared quickly.

The day I turned 16, I told my mom to take me to the restaurant in town. I applied as a server. My mom knew the owner, and he gave me a job. Training was horrible. I felt so worthless, but in the back of my mind I knew I had to push through so I could earn some money. My dad is a very proud man and not being able to provide for his family like he was meant to, in his eyes, put a lot of strain on the family. The fact that my mom would send money to my brother when he asked, didn't make things any easier. Other family chipped in and help us as well when needed. My days flew past like crazy. For me life was school, sport, work, a little sleep and repeat. At least I could buy some food for the house. I knew my dad would never take money from me, so I either bought some groceries or gave money to Mom.

It was a time in life where we realized we were nothing without God. When we had it all, we slipped up and relied on our own abilities to provide and that meant we didn't have to rely on God as a provider. Without thinking about it, we spend less and less time with God when all was going well. We never made choices without God, but the move to Klerksdorp was a selfish move. It was taking the word of a family member and going after it without considering what God wanted us to do. Chasing bigger material things, things we didn't need and leaving behind happiness, love and worth.

How did we get out of the situation, you might ask?

It wasn't overnight; it wasn't easy, and it was exhausting. We turned back to God; we prayed more; we forgave more, and we trusted more.

My dad got a call from a company in the Northern Cape for an interview. His friend referred him when he moved there. My dad flew to Upington at their expense and to make a long story short, my dad ended up getting the job. The family was pulled out of the hole we called "Klersdorp" and started over in the middle of nowhere close to the border of Namibia. I finished my Grade 12 in Klerksdorp and then followed my parents to the farm. Life got so much better out there. My parents paid off all their debt and got their name cleared. I studied Travel and Tourism management and spend years facilitating camps with extreme adventures activities on the opposite end of South Africa. Life took me back to my parents and my journey took a completely new direction, again. I went back to university and studied teaching. During that time I was appointed as the youth leader at church and what a blessed time it was.

(4 Years again in one town)

But my journey only started there. I was privileged enough to then work abroad. Learning a lot about myself and doing my best to never forget how I survived what would break others.

PURPOSE OF THE STORY

The way I see it, we do serve a 'jealous' God. Our family made the mistake of putting other things above God and we had to bear the consequences, but this was not the main purpose of me sharing this personal story. The purpose comes for two groups.

Firstly, parents: As much as children can adjust and continue when the mat gets pulled from under their feet, keep in mind they are just children. Safety and stability along with family time and love means a lot more than money and experience. Don't get me wrong, my parents did the best they could and I thank God I have parents that will fight with everything they have to take care of their family, but my question will always linger... What if we stayed and didn't move our entire lives for bigger and better things? As much as I know my parents wanted to make a decision that's best, I don't know if they considered the impact their choice would have on their children. The problem with having more is that you always want more.

Secondly, children: Your parents remain your parents. You might not agree with everything they do and choose, but the only thing you as a kid should do is support their decision and respect it. Even if it goes bad, even if what they say or promise never pans out, give them the benefit of the doubt. You didn't choose your parents, but you have the choice to respect, love and trust them. Yes, I know sometimes you find parents that make horrible decisions and put their children in danger, but then you need to trust in our higher authority that He will provide a solution.

With all this being said, as a child, now grown up, I had the choice of either letting that experience ruin any future I have or learn from it and do better. We don't live long enough to make all the mistakes ourselves, which is why we have to learn from mistakes others make. My parents made a choice, but that doesn't take away all the good they did, all the sacrifices they made for us and all the love they gave us. One choice should never define someone.

Be grateful for what you have and never take it for granted. You never know when you might lose it. And lastly, always remember that family comes first. Your job won't fill your heart with joy like the smile of your kid on the sports field achieving what they have always wanted to. The best feeling in the world is looking to the sideline and see your parents cheering you on. Remember that.

Yesterday's Farewell, Tomorrow's Embrace

The choices we make compile our whole existence.

From saying something to someone you love, to keeping quiet and forgiving.

From swallowing another shot to saying no.

From believing everything everyone says to you, to knowing the difference between a lie and the truth.

Every situation you find yourself in gives you a list of choices to make. Even loving someone is a choice. How you choose to show love makes you different from others. The motivation you choose to guide you, makes you different from others. How you choose to react to situations with loved ones, makes you different. It all comes down to a choice or choices you need to make. Even ignoring it is a choice.

From staying positive to seeing the negativity in everything.

From clearing your name to stepping back.

From working a second job to making debt.

Whether you feel you can't handle something or decide to stand up and conquer your fears, it will be your choice. Sometimes stepping back and choosing your battles becomes the biggest choice to make. Standing up as a family when all seems lost is a choice.

You need to know that choices will always be a part of your life. You can't hide from them. You can't run from them. You might as well face them and make the best possible choice you can.

In all of these situations people made choices, some hurt others, some hurt themselves, but in all of them, the people involved made the ultimate decision: Change, grow, heal.

I hope you will choose to say farewell to all the bad choices you made in the past and make the ultimate decision yourself. May you know you are not alone. May you see how wonderfully you were made and may you become who you were made to be.